Armadi

Sarah Ko

methuen | drama

LONDON • NEW YORK • OXFORD • NEW DELHI • SYDNEY

METHUEN DRAMA
Bloomsbury Publishing Plc
50 Bedford Square, London, WC1B 3DP, UK
1385 Broadway, New York, NY 10018, USA

BLOOMSBURY, METHUEN DRAMA and the Methuen Drama logo are trademarks of Bloomsbury Publishing Plc

First published in Great Britain 2019

Cover design: Ben Anslow

Artwork © Lewis Dace

A catalogue record for this book is available from the British Library.

A catalog record for this book is available from the Library of Congress.

ISBN: PB: 978-1-350-13815-5
ePDF: 978-1-350-13816-2
eBook: 978-1-350-13817-9

Series: Modern Plays

Typeset by Mark Heslington Ltd, Scarborough, North Yorkshire
Printed and bound in Great Britain

To find out more about our authors and books visit www.bloomsbury.com and sign up for our newsletters.

Armadillo

Written by Sarah Kosar

Cast

Sam	**Michelle Fox**
John	**Mark Quartley**
Scotty	**Nima Taleghani**

Credits

Writer	**Sarah Kosar**
Director	**Sara Joyce**
Designer	**Jasmine Swan**
Lighting Designer	**Jessica Hung Han Yun**
Composer and Sound Designer	**Anna Clock**
Video Designer	**Ash J Woodward**
Movement Director	**James Berkery**
Casting Director	**Sophie Holland CSA**
Production Manager	**Jack Greenyer**
Stage Manager	**Amber Skye Reece-Greenhalgh**
Song Cover Arrangement and Performance	**Rebecca Lucy Taylor**

Cast from Media Recordings

Rebecca Roberts	**Siobhán McSweeney**
Kristy Cooper	**Hannah Morrish**
Bernie Jordan	**David Shelley**
Detective Cunningham	**Cyril Nri**
Cindy Jordan	**Lu Corfield**
Dorothy Sugar	**Ann Queensberry**
Beard	**Scott Karim**
Miss Winnie	**Ashley McGuire**
Jeff Bergman	**Sean Hart**

First produced by The Yard Theatre, 30 May 2019.

The first production of *Armadillo* was supported by Arts Council England.

Michelle Fox | SAM

Theatre includes: *Translations*, *If We Were Older* (National Theatre); *Medea* (Bristol Old Vic), King Lear (Bristol Old Vic).

Television and film includes: *A Very English Scandal* (BBC), *Overshadowed* (Rollem Productions), *Casualty* (BBC), *Doctors* (BBC).

Mark Quartley | JOHN

Theatre includes: *Maydays*, *The Tempest*, *Written on the Heart*, *Measure for Measure* (RSC); *Strife* (Chichester Festival Theatre); *Another Country*, *Macbeth* (Trafalgar Studios); *Ghosts* (Rose Theatre); *Private Peaceful* (Theatre Royal Haymarket, Greenwich Theatre); *The Tempest* (Theatre Royal Bath); *A Midsummer Night's Dream* (Globe Theatre)

Television and film includes: *Criminal* (Netflix), *Shamed* (Channel 4), *Hoff the Record* (Dave), *In the Club* (BBC), *Cuffs* (BBC), *Siblings* (BBC), *Vera* (ITV).

Nima Taleghani | SCOTTY

Theatre includes: *The Merry Wives of Windsor*, *Romeo and Juliet* (RSC); *Laika, The Iron Man* (Unicorn Theatre); *Summit* (Fuel Theatre); *The Plough and the Stars* (Abbey Theatre/US Tour); *Mercury Fur* (Middle Child/Hull Truck); *The White Whale* (Slung Low).

Television and film includes: *Hatton Garden* (ITV), *Dublin Oldschool* (Element), *90 Minutes* (El Capitan), *Casualty* (BBC).

Sarah Kosar | Writer

Sarah is an internationally produced and published playwright. She was one of the Old Vic 12 in 2017/2018 and is the recipient of an Exceptional Promise in Playwriting visa.

Theatre includes: *Mumburger* (off the WALL productions, Carnegie Stage – American premiere; Old Red Lion, The Archivist's Gallery – London); *Our Name Is Not John* (Old Vic 12 2017/2018 reading, Old Vic); *Hot Dog* (The Last Refuge – London, Thinking Cap Theatre – American premiere); *Spaghetti Ocean* (Live Lunch reading, Royal Court); *Big Body, Tiny Head* (short audio play, Royal Court); *Butter*

Brain (commission – Young and Talented, Broadway Theatre/Theatre Royal Stratford East); *Human Suit* (First Drafts reading at The Yard, longlisted for Bruntwood Prize for Playwriting).

Sarah holds an MA in Writing for Stage and Broadcast Media from the Royal Central School of Speech and Drama. She also has a BA in Theatre and a BA in Film from Penn State University.

She works full-time as the Director of Talent at music-tech start-up ROLI in Dalston, London.

Sara Joyce | Director

Sara most recently directed *Dust* by Milly Thomas (Soho Theatre, Trafalgar Studios); *Hunch* by Kate Kennedy (Assembly, Edinburgh); *Best Life* by Tamar Broadbent (Underbelly, Edinburgh). Other directing credits include *Scar Test* by Hannah Khalil (Soho Theatre); *The Win Bin* by Kate Kennedy, *Three Short Beckett Plays* by Samuel Beckett (Old Red Lion Theatre).

Sara is an Associate Artist with Pan Pan Theatre Company. She was a director with Old Vic 12, Resident Director at Almeida Theatre and Resident Assistant Director at Soho Theatre.

Sara was shortlisted for the KSF Emerging Artist Award, is a recipient of the Deutsche Bank Award for Creative Enterprises and received an Off West End nomination for Best Director. She studied Drama and Theatre at Trinity College, Dublin and trained at École Jacques Lecoq.

Jasmine Swan | Designer

Theatre credits as designer include: *Scoring a Century* (British Youth Opera); *Sonny* (Arts Educational Schools); *The Amber Trap* (Damsel Productions at Theatre503); *The Tide Jetty* (Eastern Angles); *Eden* (Hampstead Theatre); *Sex Sex Men Men* (Pecs Drag Kings at The Yard); *Chutney* (Flux Theatre at The Bunker) – nominated for an Off West End Award for Best Set Design; *Lost Boys New Town* (National Youth Theatre); *Women in Power* (Nuffield Southampton Theatres & Oxford Playhouse); *Medusa* (NST Studio); *Son of Rambow* (The Other Palace); *Sleuth* (ZoieLogic Dance Theatre); *Much Ado About Nothing*, *Dungeness*, *Love & Information* (Nuffield Southampton Youth Theatre); *Cabaret* (Westminster School); *Hanna* (Arcola Theatre); *The Passing of the Third Floor Back* (Finborough Theatre); *Hyem* (Theatre503); *Who's*

Afraid of the Working Class? (Unity Theatre); *The Wonderful World of Dissocia* (Liverpool Playhouse Studio).

Jasmine was a finalist in the Linbury Prize for Stage Design 2017 and was multiple nominated for Best Designer in The Stage Debut Awards 2018 for her designs at: Theatre503, Finborough Theatre and the Arcola Theatre. She was the Laboratory Associate Designer for Nuffield Southampton Theatres 2017/18. She trained at Liverpool Institute for Performing Arts, where she also received the Ede & Ravenscroft Prize for Creative and Technical Excellence (2016).

Jessica Hung Han Yun | Lighting Designer

Jessica is a lighting designer working in theatre.

Theatre credits include: *The Party's Over* (Nonsuch Theatre Company); *Becoming Shades* (Chivaree Circus); *Hive City Legacy* (Hot Brown Honey/Roundhouse); *Nine Foot Nine* (Sleepless Theatre/ Bunka); *One* (Bert & Nasi); *The Human Voice* (Gate Theatre); *Forgotten* (Yellow Earth & Moongate/Arcola Theatre); *Cuckoo* (Metal Rabbit Productions/Soho Theatre); *Snowflake* (Arts Old Fire Station); *Dear Elizabeth* (Gate Theatre); *Equus* (Theatre Royal Stratford East & English Touring Theatre); *Pah-La* (Royal Court Theatre).

Anna Clock | Composer and Sound Designer

Anna is a composer, sound designer and cellist working across theatre, film, radio and installation. Website: *www.annaclock.com*.

Recent projects include: *Fighter* (Stratford Circus Arts Centre); *Looking Forward* (Battersea Arts Centre); *Soft Animals* (Soho Theatre); *The Butterfly Lion* (Barn Theatre); *Fatty Fat Fat* (Camden Roundhouse; Edinburgh); *Work Bitch*, *Miss Fortunate*, *Admin* (VAULT Festival); *Twelfth Night* (Southwark Playhouse); *Pomona*, *Punk Rock* (New Diorama Theatre); *Bury the Dead* (Finborough); *Fabric* (Soho Theatre & community spaces tour); *Katie Johnstone*; *In the Night Time, [BLANK]* (Orange Tree Theatre); *Overexposed* (V&A Museum); *Uncensored* (Haymarket Theatre Royal); *Songlines* (Edinburgh & HighTide Festivals, regional tour); *Finding Fassbender* (VAULT, Edinburgh & HighTide Festivals). In 2018 Anna was artist in residence at SPINE Festival Borough of Harrow and Sirius Arts Centre.

Anna studied Music Composition and English Literature at Trinity College Dublin and cello performance at the Royal Irish Academy of Music, and holds an MA in Advanced Theatre Practice from the Royal Central School of Speech and Drama.

Ash J Woodward | Video Designer

Ash is an award-winning designer specialising in video and projection design for live performance.

Recent theatre credits include: *Harry Potter and the Cursed Child* (London, New York, Australia); *The Cunning Little Vixen* (Royal Opera House/Royal Ballet School); *The Divide* (Old Vic); *Bletchley Park Hut 11a* (Bletchley Park); *Molly* (Squint).

Animation and associate designer credits include: *Mean Girls the Musical* (Broadway); *Frozen the Musical* (Broadway); *The Curious Incident of the Dog in the Night-Time* (NT); *The Tempest* (RSC); *Bat Out of Hell* (London Coliseum); *A Dog's Heart* (De Nationale Opera).

Other senior designer credits include: *Jess Glynne Arena Tour 2018* (UK tour); *Years and Years Arena Tour 2018* (UK tour); *You Say You Want a Revolution* (V&A); *Rolling Stones: Exhibitionism* (Saatchi Gallery).

James Berkery | Movement Director

James trained at CSN Dance, Ireland and Bird College Conservatoire for Dance and Musical Theatre (DaDA Scholarship).

Theatre credits include: *Notre Dame* (Alexandra Theatre, Chichester); *Shadow Kingdoms* (Theatre503); *Tiger* (Network Theatre); *Revolutionary* (Tou Scene, Norway); *Gulliver's Travels* (Alexandra Theatre); *You Me Bum Bum Train* (Foyles, Charing CrossRoad).

Film and television credits include: *Toni_With_An_I* (BBC Four & BFI Born Digital); *Quest for Fire* (76 Ltd); *Leash* (Reel Issue Films); *Four Quartets* (4Q Films & Pecadillo Pictures).

Other credits: Puma, Nike, Topshop and Casehub (commercials); Girli, Nina Nesbitt, The Fratellis, Anna of the North and Sara Hartman (music videos).

Associate/assistant credits include: Sting's *The Last Ship* (Toronto); Stiles and Drewe's *The Three Little Pigs* (international tour – Kenny Wax Productions); *Tales of Hoffman* (English Touring Opera); *The Threepenny Opera* (Royal Academy of Music).

Sophie Holland CSA | Casting Director

Representation: ICM (US) Shephard Management (UK).

Film and television credits include: *The Witcher* (Netflix); *Madiba* (BET); *The Indian Detective* (Netflix/Big Light); *Dixi* (CBBC); *Down a Dark Hall* (Lionsgate); *WW1: The Final Hours* (BBC); as UK casting director: *Sweet Bitter* (Lionsgate).

Theatre credits include: *Against* (Almeida Theatre); *Unfaithful* (Found 111); *The Odyssey*, *The Iliad* (Almeida Theatre); *Punkplay* (Southwark Playhouse).

Jack Greenyer | Production Manager

Jack completed his training on the Royal Central School of Speech and Drama's BA Theatre Practice: Technical and Production Management course. He has since been working with theatre companies such as Complicite, National Youth Theatre, The Yard Theatre, Soho Theatre, Tiata Fahodzi and Big House Theatre Company. He continues his commitment to help creative practitioners make the most of their spaces through his work with his company Infinity Technical & Production Services

Amber Skye Reece-Greenhalgh | Stage Manager

Amber is a graduate of Guildhall School of Music and Drama, where she trained in Stage Management. She has recently worked as the stage manager for *Eden* at Hampstead Theatre and costume supervisor/assistant stage manager for *Seussical* at Southwark Playhouse. Other work includes stage manager for *Brass the Musical* at the Union Theatre and deputy stage manager for *Brink* at the Royal Exchange Studio in Manchester.

The Yard Theatre

In 2011 a group of volunteers, led by Jay Miller, converted a disused warehouse in Hackney Wick into a theatre, bar and kitchen. We called it The Yard. Due to be here for 3 months, we are still here 8 years later and, as recognition of our success, in 2018 The Yard joined the Arts Council's National Portfolio.

The Yard provides a safe space for artists to grow new ideas, and for audiences to access outstanding new work. A multi-award-winning theatre described as *'One of London's most essential theatres'* (Lyn Gardner, *The Guardian*), The Yard is committed to:

– Discovering and developing new artists.

– Exposing stories from the edges of society.

– Interrogating the process of writing for performance.

In an area buzzing with artists and potential, The Yard has rapidly established itself as a theatrical necessity, with a reputation for upending theatrical tradition and injecting creativity and fearlessness into wider contemporary culture. We've supported artists to produce ambitious new work that communicates contemporary, unheard stories and ideas in new, innovative theatrical forms. Producing bold, politically charged, unapologetically live new work, our success has led to two transfers to the National Theatre, international tours and partnerships with theatres including the Royal Court and Young Vic. Through our ability to identify artists and inspire new work, The Yard has become a leader in the future of theatre.

'It's a beacon of exciting, progressive new work in theatre-poor east London and a real model for what a theatre can and should be in the twenty-first century' Time Out

The Yard is also one of London's most exciting late-night venues.

We're fully independent and aim to provide a platform for some of London's most exciting collectives, DJs, performers and artists, focussing on events organised by and for those who find themselves under-represented in London's cultural landscape. We host over 100 late-night events each year which fill our bar space with people dancing until the early hours.

The Yard is also a key part of the fabric of Hackney Wick, offering a local programme which ensures that young people have access to the arts. The Yard manages two community centres in the local area – Hub67 and The Hall, from which we deliver innovative, creative activity for local residents.

Recent productions include:

The Crucible written by Arthur Miller, directed by Jay Miller (2019) ('A brilliantly intense vision of Miller's witchcraft classic' ★★★★★ Evening Standard).

A New and Better You written by Joe Harbot, directed by Cheryl Gallacher (2018) ('Restless and brave' ★★★★ The Guardian).

Buggy Baby written by Josh Azouz, directed by Ned Bennett (2018) ('A theatrical rollercoaster … extraordinary' ★★★★★ WhatsOnStage).

This Beautiful Future written by Rita Kalnejais, directed by Jay Miller (2017) ('Nothing short of mesmerising' ★★★★★ The Stage).

Removal Men written by M. J. Harding, with Jay Miller (2016) ('Mesmerically intense' ★★★★ Time Out).

LINES written by Pamela Carter, directed by Jay Miller (2015) ('directed with finesse by The Yard's properly talented artistic director Jay Miller' ★★★★ Time Out).

The Mikvah Project written by Josh Azouz (2015), directed by Jay Miller ('Every moment feels rich with meaning' ★★★★ Time Out).

Beyond Caring by Alexander Zeldin (2014) ('quietly devastating' ★★★★ The Guardian).

Artistic Director – Jay Miller
Executive Director – Sam Hansford
Finance and Operations Manager – Jack Haynes
Theatre Producer – Ashleigh Wheeler
Marketing and Communications Manager – Alex Krook
Local Producer – Katherine Igoe-Ewer

Music and Events Producer – Anjali Prashar-Savoie
Assistant Producer – Lara Tysseling
Development Officer – Gareth Cutter
Finance and Administration Assistant – Kellie Grogan
Marketing & Box Office Assistant – Kia Noakes
Theatre Technician – James Dawson
Front of House Manager – Olivia Carr-Archer
Bar and Venue Manager – Felix Yoosefinejad
Assistant Bar and Venue Manager – Elinor Wood
Bar Duty Manager – Max Hesmondhalgh
Board – Yenny Chong, Greg Delaney, Antony Gummett, Jay Miller, Ben Rogers, Robin Saphra, Nick Starr (Chair), Anna Vaughan, Carolyn Ward

Supporters

Friends and Guardians

Thank you to all our Friends and Guardians including:

Mike Anderson
Francesco Curto & Chantal Rivest
The David Pearlman Charitable Foundation
Greg Delaney
Ian & Janet Edmondson
Nick Hytner
Melanie Johnson
Joanna Kennedy
Ben Rogers
Robin Saphra
Clive & Sally Sherling
Studio Bark
Anna Vaughan & Dan Fletcher
Archie Ward
Carolyn Ward
Hyman Wolanski
Stephanie Yeap

And all our supporters who prefer to remain anonymous

Corporate Supporters

BRISTOWS

THE COLLECTIVE

Thanks

Thank you to everyone who helped us make *Armadillo*. We couldn't have done it without you.

We would like to thank: Alex Austin, William Barwick, Mark Field, David Mumeni, Danielle Vitalis, Rose Wardlaw, Susanna Davies-Crook, Doireann May White, Hannah Partis-Jennings, Denise Wood, Tom Wright and Maria from Leyton Great Hall.

Acknowledgements

Thank you to Jay Miller and The Yard for pulling the trigger on *Armadillo*. Having your play produced by one of your favourite theatres is an indescribable feeling.

To my best friend, Axel Bernard who has been there since I started writing this play in 2013. Thanks for sitting on the couch and talking about my plays with me for hours on end, giving so many precise, hilarious and helpful notes (in my Google Docs!), and being a total generous and all-in friend and collaborator. For making me laugh and being so invested in my writing when you didn't have to be. For knowing how to switch me off. You match my weird and I love being fucking idiots together. Big love to you, bud.

To my friend and director, Sara Joyce, for her true creative collaboration, partnership and continuous waves of inspiration. Thank you for making me a better writer through this process and making *Armadillo* the play it is. For our early 7.30 a.m. meetings, badass voice notes and becoming incredible friends through the process. I can't wait to work with you again. SJSK!

To my husband, Sam McKown, for going shooting with me. For staying up late with me even when I didn't know you were awake, just to make sure I was OK and able to make a writing deadline before an early start at work. For somehow staying married to me even when I was sleeping with a Nerf gun under my pillow (for way too long) and subsequently firing it around the house at you in the name of research. I love you.

To the Yard Theatre, with special thanks to Jay Miller, Ashleigh Wheeler, Sam Hansford, Lara Tysseling, Alex Krook and the rest of the team. Your belief in me, the team and the play has meant the world. It's been an absolute privilege to work with all of you.

To Playdate, my gang of writers, with whom I'll always share the highs and lows of a writing career. My deep love and admiration to you all: Isley Lynn, Christopher Adams, David Ralf, Poppy Corbett, Stephen Laughton and Vinay Patel.

The entire *Armadillo* team have brought so much of themselves to this play and have made it so much better than I ever could have on my own. I'm still pinching myself that I've gotten to work with each of you: Sara Joyce, Michelle Fox, Mark Quarterly, Nima Teleghani, Jasmine Swan, James Berkery, Anna Clock, Ash Woodward, Amber Skye Reece-Greenhalgh, Jessica Hun Hang Yun, Alastair Armstrong, James Dawson, Jack Greenyer, Sophie Holland, Finnian Tweed, Siobhán McSweeney, Hannah Morrish, David Shelley, Cyril Nri, Lu Corfield, Ann Queensberry, Ashley McGuire, Sean Hart, Rebecca Lucy Taylor and Scott Karim.

To my parents Phyllis and John, family and hometown of Butler, Pennsylvania. Shout out to Louise Stephens for being the Beyoncé of dramaturgy and always inspiring me to push myself and my writing as far as it can go over the years. Thank you to Tom Wright, Georgia Gatti and all at the Old Vic for pairing Sara Joyce and me together as part of Old Vic 12 on my play *Our Name is Not John*. You nailed the match making! Thank you to Emily Hickman, Georgie Smith and The Agency for all of their support and originally signing me after reading *Armadillo* back in 2013. Thanks to Dom O'Hanlon and all at Methuen Drama (my dream publisher). Thanks to Corey Harrower, Malina Leslie, Mimi Smith, Tahmima Anam and all my colleagues at ROLI for being a joy to work with every day.

A huge appreciation to the following people that have been a part of the development of *Armadillo*: Tom Hughes, Debbie Hannan, Tommo Fowler, Charlotte Peters, Rosie Wyatt, Kim Pearce, Bethany Pitts, Lucy Morrison, Molly Roberts, Leo Butler, Larner Wallace-Taylor, Louise Stephens, Chris Thompson, Tom Gordon, Tim Allsop, Rikki Lawton, Max Bowden, Alex Austin, Mark Field, Rose Wardlow, Danielle Vitalis, David Mumeni, William Barwick, Charlotte Fraser.

And finally to everyone who has never had their trauma or pain taken seriously. There is no hierarchy: pain is pain and we all walk around with it. I see you.

Sarah Kosar

Armadillo

To my best friend, Axel.

To my husband, Sam.

You make life more fun.

Characters

Sam
John
Scotty

On Television/Voiceovers

Rebecca Roberts
Kristy Cooper
Bernie Jordan
Detective Cunningham
Cindy Jordan
Dorothy Sugar
Beard
Miss Winnie
Jeff Bergman

Setting

Butler, Pennsylvania, a small town on the East Coast of America.

Time

The first scene is five months earlier and the rest of the play takes place over eleven days.

Dialogue

/ indicates the point at which the character is interrupted by the subsequent speaker.

A character's name without dialogue following it suggests a desire but failure to speak.

The white space between dialogue suggests the time it may take for a character to respond.

Scene One

Sam *and* **John***'s bedroom.*

It is morning and the sun is shining.

They prepare to have sex the way they always do.

Sam *dances with something but we can't see what it is.*

Sam You want it?

John Yeah.

She pulls it away.

Sam It feels great.

Husband.

John Then you better give it to me, Wife.

Sam You sound weird when you say it. Wife. Wifffe.

John Get used to it. Wife.

She reveals what she's holding – oh, it's a gun.

She dances with the gun and then gets on top of **John**. *He puts her hand over his on the gun. They kiss. They roll over and under each other.*

John Oh, Sam.

Sam Right here.

John You gonna / make me.

Sam Oh yeah.

He caresses her body with the gun.

They kiss passionately and start to have sex.

He is holding the gun.

The gun goes off.

A bullet goes into **Sam**'*s shoulder.*

She bleeds.

She bleeds more.

Announcement Please turn off your mobile phones and all other devices at this time. Please note there will be repeated loud gunshots in this performance. The beautiful girls, the beautiful girls, he said. I'm coming for you. I'll have you. I'll hurt you.

Time passes.

Sam *lays in the hospital room.*

John The doctor said you can go home in about a week. You should get full movement in your shoulder back which is a miracle.

Sam We're done.

No more guns, John.

John Yeah, we can talk about it.

Time passes.

Sam *and* **John** *have a box of their guns and accessories all packed up.*

Sam I will never shoot a gun again.

John I will never shoot a gun again.

I will never shoot a gun again.

Sam I will not have guns in the house or use them outside.

John I will not have guns in the house or use them outside.

Sam *and* **John** We'll go totally, totally without.

Sam Forever.

John *takes all the guns and accessories out of the house.*

Time passes.

Sam *sits and tries to breathe normally. She fails.*

Time passes.

John *throws his video-game controller against the wall.*

Time passes.

Sam *screams.*

John I can't think. About anything. But –

She screams more.

Sam Scream!

He screams. They scream together.

Time passes.

He brings a bunch of Nerf guns into the house.

John I got them!

She takes one of the Nerf guns and shoots him with it.

They laugh.

They play.

Time passes.

They do a gun drill together with the Nerf guns.

Time passes.

They try to have sex with the Nerf guns.

It's not the same. It doesn't work.

Time passes.

They sit on the couch.

Sam . . . We're still having fun, aren't we?

John Yeah, more fun.

Sam More fun.

John . . . with no guns.

Sam Exactly. No guns.

John More fun.

Scene Two

Day One, Night (Wednesday)

Five months later.

Sam *and* **John** *sit on their bed and watch the news.*

Rebecca Roberts Again, if you have just joined us, breaking news, the family of a teenage girl missing in Butler since yesterday evening have made an emotional appeal for help to find her. Kristy Cooper has the latest.

John I'm having a / beer.

Sam / Shhh, listen!

Kristy Cooper Thank you, Rebecca. Thirteen-year-old Jessica Jordan was last seen Tuesday evening at the Jordan family home on The Boulevard. According to her older sister, Chloe Jordan, Jessica went to her room, following an argument they had at 7 p.m. The last Snapchat Jessica shared was shortly before the argument began. The video shows Chloe and Jessica singing Ariana Grande and juggling oranges in their family kitchen. Chloe didn't realise that Jessica was no longer in the house until 11 p.m. when her parents came back from dinner at a family friend's home. Jessica's phone was found on the floor of her bedroom.

Bernie Jordan Your Mom, and I and Chloe and all, all of us miss you very much, your loud laugh and beautiful long hair. I even brought your favourite snack, a bag of goldfish here with me today. We love you to the moon and I – I – I can't stop crying, I'm sorry.

John *tries to pull* **Sam** *away from the TV but fails.*

Detective Cunningham Teenagers don't leave their phones behind. I've got a kid and he's glued to it. We've opened up a criminal investigation and the Butler Township Police Department are one of the good – best in the country. We're aware of a bulk milk purchase, clearing out all the milk, even the coconut kind, in the Butler Walmart the hour before Jessica went missing so we're following that lead.

Cindy Jordan Jessie. Jessie. Don't be scared. You're coming home. And we'll have our shopping date.

Dorothy Sugar It was a full moon that night, something – the energy wasn't right. I heard a car speed past around 8 p.m. when I was meditating – we have a nice neighbourhood, I thought . . . we all wave hi to each other.

Kristy Cooper You can visit the Facebook Event 'The Search for Jessica Jordan' to join the community search tomorrow. Butler Township Police are alerting the public to come forward with any information. Rebecca, back to you.

Whilst **Sam** *is engrossed in the news,* **John** *hides her Nerf gun from her.*

He turns the TV off.

Sam Fuck.

Babe, have you seen my –

John We shouldn't have watched / it.

Sam It's been a day and there's a search party?

John

Sam I'm fine. Stop with that face.

He lies down.

Sam You're going to sleep?

John Come on, I'm cold.

She looks at her phone.

Sam One sec.

John I'll give you a back rub if you give me a back rub?

Sam 1,678 people are already confirmed on the Facebook Event #BringJessicaJordanHome. The mom's made a / website.

John Let's go to sleep.

Sam The Boulevard is / only up the hill.

John Well, we could do the breathing exercises / together.

Sam I'm not having a panic attack, I'm just sharing what I'm reading. I'm not tired.

John Oooohkay. Goodnight, my little arm. Wake me up / if you need me.

Sam Stop worrying about me.

She waits for him to fall asleep and then she starts to look for the Nerf gun under the bed, in drawers, and anywhere she can. She's not panicking: don't panic.

There is a loud knock on the door.

John Ah! What's that?

She starts to go into a drill with an imaginary gun.

He opens the front door. It is **Scotty** *with a big bag and a gun in his hands.*

Scotty Hey / losers!

Sam Jesus. Scotty. Are you okay?

Scotty That's my greeting?

Sam Sorry. Hey.

She gives **Scotty** *a hug.*

Scotty Can I come in?

John Why do you have a gun?

He blocks **Scotty** *from entering.*

Scotty Hey, Johnny.

John No guns.

Scotty Yes guns!

Sam Come in.

John We have rules and we're going through – / you're not bringing those.

Sam *makes way for* **Scotty** *to come in with his guns.*

Scotty You're not over that yet?

Sam Where have you been?

Scotty Kicked out of the trailer. Landlord took my stash. Can I stay?

Sam Yeah, 'course. God, that's awful.

She scratches at her shoulder wound.

Scotty Lemme see that scar.

Sam *shows him the wound. It's definitely not healed.*

Sam It's not that / interesting.

John She's just gotten full movement / back thank God.

Sam It was just kind of sore /

John Lots more physical therapy to – You're not bringing those in.

Scotty But look how shiny they are. You still shooting turkeys?

Turkey down. Turkey down! Turkey dead.

John I bet your parents miss you.

Scotty And you don't? This angelic face?

Sam Of course / we do.

John We both have work in the morning / and need to –

Scotty We can all sleep when we're dead.

John We'll take the guns to the storage locker now and then you can stay. For a / couple nights.

Sam However long you want. Actually we'll drop them off before work tomorrow.

John Babe, I don't mind taking them.

Sam He just got here.

John *pats* **Scotty** *down for guns. He finds one, and then another and then a lot more. He takes his bags and the guns.*

Scotty This is worse than walking into the high school.

Sam Is the couch okay? Watch whatever.

Scotty Porn cool?

Sam

Scotty I'm kidding.

Sam So what was the landlord's problem? Sounds like a dick.

Scotty I ran. He's slow, I'm in the clear.

John Jesus / Scotty.

Scotty Remember running from those guys in Memorial Park and we raced around the water tower? You want a joint?

John . . . No.

Scotty Good, 'cause I wasn't gonna give you one.

Sam Why don't you answer your phone? It's been / months.

Scotty I gotta keep trashing them. Sorry.

Sam Well, it's fucking annoying.

Scotty News – I've got a new girlfriend. She's awesome.

John Younger than the last one?

Scotty No. She's eighteen . . . and three-quarters.

He reaches for a craft beer in the fridge.

John Hey, that's mine. Take the Heineken if you have to.

Scotty *starts to drink* **John**'s *craft beer.*

Scotty I'll buy you another.

Scotty *spots* **Sam** *trying to touch his bag of guns and grabs the gun he hid in the front of his trousers. He puts the safety lock on and throws the gun in the air to* **Sam**. *As she reaches for it,* **John** *catches it and puts it in the duffle bag.*

John Don't.

Sam Yeah, don't.

Scene Three

Day Two, Morning (Thursday)

Sam *and* **John**'s *bedroom.*

Sam *watches* **John** *sleep all night. She gets really close to his face and waits for him to open his eyes.*

Sam (*whispers*) John, John, John / John, John.

John Jesus!

Sam I still can't find it.

Where is it?

John I don't / know.

Sam C'mon, you love giving things new homes. Here, deodorant, why don't you move to the bottom of Sam's underwear drawer?

John Do you need it right now? The answer is / no.

Sam Ah! Sam's thongs, it makes total sense to be with the board games. You took my socks this week already / so –

John You kept wearing them without washing them.

Sam And then you threw them away /

John Because they smelled like they died.

Why are you looking at me like that?

Sam Like what?

John Like a criminal.

Is it the missing girl? I get / it if –

Sam No it was before that and before Scotty came.

John Ah, did he really show up last night?

Sam Yes, you're changing the subject.

John I'm changing the locks.

Sam That's not funny.

John I don't want him staying here if he's still – he brought a lot of guns and we know they're not / good for us.

Sam They weren't even affecting me /

John What about / me?

Sam You're still not answering my question.

John You know when I see the guys walking into the bar with their Glock19s and Ruger LCPs, I don't feel anything anymore.

Sam That's why you held the Glock?

John They handed it to me. What was I gonna say?

Sam We said no holding. You lied and then I just see a picture pop up / online.

John I had to – it was annual hunters' night.

Sam You're not a hunter / anymore!

John I know I'm / not!

Sam Shhh! Get on your knees. C'mon. Look!

They crawl around. He tries to lead her away from the bed.

John Okay I'll look for a minute but if I'm late / that's not –

Sam I know, you're trying to get manager /

John Well, what do I get if I find it?

Sam Why do you always have to get something in order to help me?

John I don't.

Sam 'If I do the laundry, can I have a back rub?'

John If I find it, can I have a blow job?

Sam Fine.

If you find it.

John Really? You'd be ready . . .? I don't want to push anything and I respect if you're not – it's totally /

Sam *If* you find it.

John On it! That's great, babe. That's really great.

Do you think you'll have time before work?

Sam I thought you were in a hurry?

John Okay. / Okay.

Sam I'm not going unless I find it, I'll call and say I'm sick.

John You can't blow off work /

Sam I'm not going.

No. I'm / not going.

John Calm down /

Sam When you say calm down it doesn't make me want to calm down so calm down with the calm down.

John I believe in you. I love you more than anything in the world.

Sam, I love / you.

Sam But what if Scotty wasn't Scotty? We're being stupid.

John He shouldn't have brought them last night / Shhh . . . you're safe . . . let's do our breathing. Breathing in like you taught me, finger over nostril – one, two, three, four.

Sam No, it's not about / that.

John Breathe with me. Other / nostril.

Sam Trying. Okay let's . . . do the –

No gun . . .

More

fun . . .

John *and* **Sam** No gun . . . more fun.

John *and* **Sam** No gun . . . more fun.

John See. No gun . . .

Sam More fun . . .

John Gooo / ood.

Sam I'm not going outside.

John You can. And / you'll feel –

Sam I said I'm not, I'm not fucking going outside.

John I'll drive with you.

Sam You – you don't get it.

John We're not like other people. We got through it. We're thriving.

Sam I'm not – I – I – I can't breathe – I'm –

He pulls a Nerf gun from behind his pillow. He puts it to her head.

John Down on your knees!

Sam Oh my God! Oh my God! You! You fucker!

John I won! I found it! We all win!

She punches him.

Sam You fucker.

She punches him again.

John Ow! What am I supposed to do?

She grabs the Nerf gun from him.

John You can't have the Nerf gun forever! We've gotta rip the bandaid off.

Sam She's thirteen. I was thirteen. It's not as easy for me as it was for you to just . . .

John Yeah . . .

I uh, I still haven't told my grandpa I don't shoot anymore. I keep saying I have to work and can't go to the woods.

He'd stop drinking with me if he knew.

Anyways.

Now you know it's here, you can go and do your job.

She dresses the Nerf gun up in a lacey sock.

John Babe, maybe you don't dress it up . . . it's really weird.

Sam You still haven't realised your wife is weird?

She grabs the Nerf gun, puts it in her purse and leaves.

John Wait, your lunch. I made risotto.

She comes back for the risotto.

John Sam! Your car keys.

Sam I'm walking.

She goes outside. She struggles to breathe. She hides and waits for **John** *to leave the house.*

John *and* **Scotty** *leave with the guns.*

She goes back inside.

She holds her Nerf gun and goes to turn the news on.

Scene Four

Day Two, Late Afternoon (Thursday)

In the living room.

Scotty *has the TV on and half watches the news while he empties a bag of Nerf guns and hangs them around the living room. He replaces* **Sam** *and* **John**'s *photos on the wall with his own Nerf guns.*

Kristy Cooper We're here at the search party for Jessica Jordan at Butler Memorial Park, approximately two miles from the Jordan family home on The Boulevard. The response from the Butler community is overwhelming with some of the biggest companies giving their employees the day off to attend. Detective Cunningham has confirmed that volunteer police officers are travelling from across the state to help. Oh, they're handing out t-shirts with her face on it.

Beard Everyone calls me Beard. Jessica was – is – not sure what tense to use. I've always helped the Jordans out with their plumbing, painting, that stuff. Thought we better start looking so I made an event on Facebook.

Miss Winnie I've been teaching Jessica ballet since she was a grape at my school, Miss Winnie's School of Dance. I'd bang this gold cane and she'd spin until I hit it again. When I heard she was missing, I went into convulsions, I cried all the way through the McDonald's drive-through. I was wailing but I needed something to stop the sound coming out so I threw a Big Mac in there. She is so excited about her first solo I pray she can be back in time to compete – no question she'll win regionals. Oh lord, I pray.

Jeff Bergman I teach Jessica violin. I played violin too when I was her age. This is every parent's worst nightmare.

Detective Cunningham Jessica had a lot of followers on Snapchat, including quite a few adult family friends so we're looking at the likes and private messages.

Sam *comes into the living room.*

Sam Beard totally has her.

Scotty Don't you have a job?

Sam Finished early.

Cindy Jordan Chloe said to me, 'Why is Jessie's plate still at the breakfast table?' I said, 'Because she's coming back.'

Kristy Cooper Parents, we urge you to be extra cautious of your children on social media at this time. We've also been told that Chloe Jordan remembers a car speeding west down Belmont Road which may have been Jessica's abductor leaving the scene. We will keep you updated as the case develops. Back to you, Rebecca.

Sam *joins* **Scotty** *on the couch.*

Scotty You like how I made them hang in order of how much it can hold?

Sam Yeah. Very feng shui.

Sam So Beard was messaging Jessica on Snapchat. Could it be more obvious?

He grabs her phone.

Sam Hey!

Scotty My AK-47 would have been perfect for above the TV.

Listen, I wish could have shown you my new model. You'd fucking drool. Glock 21, the casing, Jesus! It's a bad boy.

Sam You try her out yet?

Scotty His name is Larry. We should go to the storage locker and give him a day out.

Sam . . . I can't.

Scotty You gonna be rude to Larry?

Sam Of course I want to but / we're –

Scotty Did you really sell them all?

Sam Yeah they paid for a big chunk of the house /

Scotty I mean it was fucking scary but you didn't lose a limb or your face and the wound ain't that bad.

He pokes at her shoulder wound.

Scotty Oh my God, it's an actual hole. Gross.

Sam Stoo / oppp.

Scotty And for the record when you post 'no gun, more fun' it's weird. Why do you think you don't get any likes?

Sam I'm not doing it for likes /

Scotty Don't you miss the sound of a real one?

He makes the sound of a gun loading.

Sam Don't be an asshole.

She turns her Nerf gun in his face and then tapes it around her hand.

Sam Kristy Cooper wants to interview me. Does it look bad if I don't do it?

Scotty It looks worse if you show up with a Nerf gun taped to your hand.

Sam She said I was a 'voice of hope and a pillar of the Butler community'.

Scotty I've been called much worse things. Like a big / thick dick.

Sam Stop – They want me to talk about how they're going to find Jessica like they found me. That everything will be fine. Like rainbows and butterflies. Everything's fine!

Scotty Say, 'My brother fucked up and looks like that Chloe bitch has too.'

Sam Scotty.

Scotty Whatever, say some shit the people want to hear. Maybe they'll give you a free gift basket.

Sam It's Channel 12, not Good Morning America.

Scotty Ya know, Genevieve said I'm the toughest guy she's ever been with.

Sam Jesus /

Scotty I drove her to take the SATs and she said she loved me. It's the real deal.

Sam You're disgusting.

Scotty What's disgusting is that you gave up your favourite thing for a man.

Sam John and I are letting you stay.

Scotty Isn't this fun? Fucking fun times, yo.

Sam You'll have a place like this too one day.

Scotty I don't want this life.

He jumps on the couch and she joins him.

Sam Let's get pizza.

Scotty Large one. Pizza Plus. Get some beer too. If I'm living here, we're drinking / and smoking.

Sam I can't drink that much during the week.

Scotty Fuck that. Cold pizza equals hangover cure. Get Hawaiian pizza. Fuckin' pineapple!

Sam Totally.

Scotty We should go to Hawaii. Get under one of those palm trees and make a fort – yeah fort! – out of those big-ass leaves. I'm going to get my licence back, then we can drive somewhere hot. Drive to wherever we need to and then jump on a plane and go to Hawaii.

Sam First, try to get your job back / and –

Scotty They didn't fire me, I quit. Google flights. For July. Book it and / I'll pay you.

Sam You never pay me back. / Maybe . . .

Scotty OKAY! Fort time.

They start to make the fort out of sheets.

Sam Do I have to talk to Kristy?

Scotty You'll probably get some free stuff becuase you were abducted. We can take sad pictures of you and post them too.

Sam No no / no.

Scotty I'll cut onions up, yo. Go on there and get it out of your system.

Sam I've never been on TV, I mean it's not even TV, it's a radio interview with Kristy but / still –

Scotty It's about time. Do it and you'll fucking rock it.

Ready?

They crawl under the fort.

Sam (*sings*) Little chickens run run run

Scotty (*sings*) Little chickens in heaven

Sam *and* **Scotty** (*sing*) Little chickens run run run
'Cause I am coming for you

John *walks in the door.*

Sam *and* **Scotty** (*sing*) Little chickens run run run
'Cause I am coming for you
Little chickens

John *takes the sheet off of the fort.* **Sam** *and* **Scotty** *scream.* **Scotty** *tries to shield* **Sam**.

Sam Intruder!

She shoots her Nerf gun at **John**.

John Ow! What's going on? Can I come in?

Scotty Do you know the handshake?

John No.

Scotty Sorry!

Sam *closes the sheets and* **John** *is left outside of the fort.*

Scene Five

Day Two, Night (Thursday)

In the living room.

Scotty (*on phone*) Can I come over?

Right. Cool, maybe tomorrow morning?

In **Sam** *and* **John***'s bedroom.* **John** *is starting to fall asleep.* **Sam** *shoots her gun at the ceiling. The Nerf bullets go up and then fall back down at her.*

John Babe, stop it.

Sam The sound's really relaxing.

John . . . Not for me.

She shoots the Nerf gun again.

Sam I don't wanna do the interview tomorrow.

John Say a few soundbites: 'I know we will all find her. I've lived / through –'

Sam But who else have they found?

John You were lucky and she will be too.

You're a survivor.

Sam I hate that word.

I know what they're doing right now. He's dressing her up. In lingerie. Nice stuff, but not too slutty. With flowers and hearts on it so she feels comfortable. He's asking her to call him 'Daddy' and she's doing it. He thinks she's the most beautiful creature ever made out of flesh. I think they're kissing. They are. She's scared, but she knows someone thinks she's beautiful. Because he tells her and he really does. She's kissing back. She doesn't like it but he's mesmerised by her. And she's looking at him looking at her. Entranced . . .

Alfred never kissed me, you know?

He pretends to be asleep.

Sam Okay, that was fast.

Are you awake? BABE?

I think I could get excited. Ya know excited excited. Can you get excited?

John Arghhh . . . I'll try.

Sam Be more committed!

John I'll do it.

Sam Under eight seconds?

John At eight seconds.

Sam Under.

John At.

Sam Under.

John At.

Sam My Nerf . . .

John (*half-heartedly*) . . . our turf!

Sam Again!

Sam *and* **John** MY NERF OUR TURF!

Sam *and* **John** MY NERF OUR TURF! GO!

They both start at the sound of one and reach for their Nerf guns in their respective bedside tables. He can't keep up.

Sam One, up, two, drawer, three, grab, four, roll, five, stay alive, six, stabilise, six, point, seven, cock, eight, prepare to FIRE

On eight she is in the correct position, he is not.

John / Sorry.

Sam Fuck!

John It was the pizza, I swear.

Sam When someone comes in to shoot you, you can't say, 'Sorry, killer, I had a lot of pizza, can you come back when I feel a little less bloated and can defend myself?'

She shoots at his head.

John Ow! I told you / too close!

Sam What if that person in the car came here in the middle of the night – there are crazy people out there / and –

He grabs the gun out of her hand and points it back at her and then quickly puts it down.

John We are stronger than what is in our hands.

Sam I know that. I know that.

John We can't have a family like this.

Sam I'm alive because Mr Corbett had a gun.

John And I shot you.

Sam It was an accident, we were both doing it /

John Sam! This isn't a debate, you could have died. I hurt / you.

Sam It's like our tattoo.

She starts to take off the bandage from her shoulder. She leans into him. He is grossed out and pulls away.

John I can't – I can't risk – I'm trying to be strong for both of us, okay? I have to – Please help me help you. You know, whatever. Whatever. I don't care, get fucking hurt.

She goes to the toilet with her Nerf gun. She gets out her phone and looks through photos of her and her old guns.

She scrolls.

John Hey, why don't we do a nice long run through the woods this weekend?

Sam I wanna stay in my PJs and not shower /

John Or kayaking?

Sam I remember when I finally came back to school, Kristy Cooper got the attention of the whole cafeteria and everyone stared at me and then she went, 'Well, well, well, look at that, Sam survived. What'd he make you do?', and then she shook her head, pretended to cry and her ponytail bounced with every breath. People started hugging her and I just stood there. Alone.

John That's uh –

I, um, one time at school, these guys said your dad looks like a grandpa. And I said that's because that is my grandpa. My dad's fucking dead.

Sam I hate kids.

Scotty said I should do the interview.

John He wants to brag to his buyers that his sister is famous.

Sam I'm not famous.

John D-list but /

Sam What's that supposed to mean?

John You're not Elizabeth Smart, Amanda Berry, Madeleine McCann you know.

Sam You think I'm D-list.

John No, no, thank God, you don't have a book deal or constant media interviews, you're not all over the internet, and this is the thing that defines you. We don't get stopped when we're getting the car washed. You're a normal person.

Sam Totally.

John You're doing a really good thing, I mean, hey, it'll help the family.

Sam You know Alfred never even kissed me?

John Thank God.

Sam Yeah.

John That would have screwed you up.

He turns off the light.

Come to bed! You're gonna have a red ring on your ass if you sit there any longer.

He goes to sleep.

She Googles 'Sam Jefferson missing'. There is nothing on her, just a reality TV star and news that she and her boyfriend split, oh and YouTube videos of a singer/songwriter that have a couple of hundred views. On the second page, there are a few articles from the Butler Eagle *that mention her as a runaway and then another small mention with a picture when she was found, confirming she was abducted.*

She Googles 'Jessica Jordan' and there are images, videos and pages and pages of results. She looks at pictures of Jessica and then at herself at thirteen. Jessica is traditionally beautiful, **Sam** *is not. She clicks between the pictures of her and Jessica. Again and again.*

Scene Six

Day Four, Late Afternoon (Saturday)

Sam *and* **John** *sit on their bed watching her interview on the 5 p.m. news. It's clear that she's not aware she's on TV. She covers up her wound. She uncovers it. She covers it.*

Kristy Cooper I'm here with Samantha Jefferson at her / home.

Sam / Hi, everyone.

Kristy Cooper Samantha was abducted in 2004 at age thirteen by predator Alfred Swartzpandel, who worked as a landscaper and handyman for the Jefferson family. Samantha was rescued following the heroic actions of her history teacher and proud firearm owner, the late Ralph Corbett, who recognised her and threatened Swartzpandel with a gun in the local Butler Walmart parking lot. Corbett intervened as Alfred instructed Samantha to load an entire grocery cart full of ketchup into the trunk. Following Swartzpandel's arrest, additional evidence was found linking Swartzpandel to the unsolved disappearances of Lisa Roberts, Whitney Spaniel, and Britney Chipperton four years earlier.

The broadcast plays a montage of photos of Lisa, Whitney, Britney, Alfred Swartzpandel and news coverage of the cases but there isn't anything about **Sam**.

Finally, **Sam***'s picture of herself at thirteen appears.* **John** *sees it and giggles.*

Kristy Cooper Well, Samantha /

Sam You can call me Sam. Thanks for having me today, Kristy.

Kristy *motions* **Sam** *to look at her and not at the camera.*

Kristy Cooper What went through your mind when you first heard Jessica was abducted and at the same age you were?

Sam I thought where the hell is my gun?! Ha, I'm joking.

Kristy Cooper Sam, you can understand this story better than any of us and offer a truly unique insight being one of the rare women that have survived a kidnapping. Why do you think you survived?

Sam Ummm . . . I was incredibly lucky and really it was thanks to Mr Corbett who recognised me, acted quickly and was a good guy with a gun.

Kristy Cooper Alfred Swartzpandel was charged with six months of jail time for your kidnapping and received three life sentences for the kidnapping and deaths of Lisa, Britney and Whitney. Alfred died four years into his sentence in jail. We often see cases that show an abductor was someone the victim already knew. Can you tell us about what happened that early fall day?

Sam Yeah, um, Alfred. He shared his chicken nuggets with me. He, uh, was our handyman and family friend. Scotty, my brother, we were home alone and he was, uh, in his room. I don't like swimming but everyone likes swimming. I wanted to try to jump in our pool. I was ready to jump, I was standing on the edge then Alfred was there. He said, 'You're beautiful.' No one ever – Knife, there was a knife, a gun and the nuggets. Um, I was screaming but Scotty's speakers, my brother's speakers were stuck – He said he'd – my hair was – we were going for more – the nuggets. Miss Ketchup – he called me that.

Kristy Cooper Thank you for opening up your heart. And now, fifteen years later, do you experience intense flashbacks or nightmares of your time with him?

Sam I'm very lucky nothing too – I, uh, manage it with the love and support of my husband and family. I lead a very boring, normal life now.

Kristy Cooper Thanks for sharing your story. Any last words you would like to say to everyone watching, including the Jordan family ahead of JDay?

Sam Oh, um . . . I –

Kristy Cooper Tomorrow, September 18th, is JDay, The Jessica Day, when we will have a vigil on Main Street and erect a statue of candles in the shape of a J that will never go out until she returns home safely.

Sam Uh, so. We need to look out for predators and make sure we – all of us – are prepared to protect ourselves. Uh, I believe, I know that Jessica will have the same happy ending as I've had. Um, I believe in hope. I'm a survivor and she will be too.

Kristy Cooper Thank you very much, Sam. And that was survivor Samantha Jefferson. Now over to Tom DeVecchio for your weekend forecast. Are we going to finally see some sun this week, Tom?

Scene Seven

Day Five, Night (Sunday)

Sam Happy JDay!

Scotty Joints, joints, joints?

Sam You didn't watch.

Scotty You're finally famous, bitch.

Sam Kristy said it was a voiceover, and then she got here with a camera crew and I look like a face for radio.

I said, 'Kristy, why didn't you tell me I was going to be on TV?'

Scotty She was such a slut in high school.

Sam And she was like, 'Don't worry about it, hun. It's complicated news business stuff, and this like will be so good for you. Therapeutic.' Then she started fake tearing up.

Scotty She blew me once you know? Two syllables: Teeth – er.

Sam That's disgusting. I can't tell you how close I was to getting my Nerf out and shooting her. I'd put some ketchup or something on the end of the darts. Shoot her, get that dress of hers all messed up. Make her actually cry.

Scotty That would have been hilarious.

Sam You're such an asshole for not watching.

She gets a phone notification and reads. He shoots his Nerf across the room.

Sam Shit, there's a video of it. I'm on the first page of Google results . . . Who watches that stuff?

She gets another notification.

Did anyone ever interview you? Did you go on TV when I was gone? Mom said they never showed my picture / but –

Scotty How long have you had that cat sitting on your stoop?

Sam Did Mom and Dad opt out of the media circus or why wasn't there / more . . .

Scotty It's cute with its moustache. Like a little Hitler.

Sam Scotty!

She takes his Nerf gun.

Did Mom and Dad try to get more attention? Did I have a vigil or a search or I – walk me through what happened.

Scotty I mean, people thought you were a runaway at first so it was delayed.

Sam What the fuck – are you serious? What about the police? No one's told me that.

Scotty They didn't call Mom and Dad back for three days. They kept leaving messages but – We made posters, we handed them out on Main Street. Me, Mom and Dad. And Aunt Judy . . .

Sam But it was Alfred, didn't you know.

Scotty Dude, we trusted him.

Sam Were there t-shirts? Did Dad bring my favourite socks to / the –

Scotty Sorry.

Sam And now everyone knows what the inside of my house looks like. Fuck. And they don't know who took her, what if there's copycats.

Scotty You're nearly thirty so probably not his type.

Sam

Scotty Heyyyyyyy, let's go find the cute cat, okay.

Sam So no one was looking for me for three days? Did everyone start looking after that? Were people looking when Mr Corbett found me?

Scotty Uh, Mom and Dad called the school about it so maybe, yeah, yeah.

Sam Alfred knew he could get away with it.

Scotty

Sam I should have gotten in the pool sooner. Couldn't have gotten me if I was swimming.

Scotty I should have got him.

Sam Remember when we did that thing after I was found? Would you do it?

She gets another notification on her phone.

Let's do it.

I'll be me. You be you? I'm gonna start over here – this is the pool.

Scotty Yeah. Okay.

She takes off her dress and is in a swimsuit, fully showing her bullet wound. He takes off his clothes and is in baggy swim trunks. He grabs a water gun off the wall. She takes her Nerf gun. She looks at him and then starts to run. They begin to role play.

Sam No. Don't. Ow! My hair. Ew ketchup! Leave me alone! Scooottttty! HELP! Don't take me. Don't take me. Don't take me. Don't take me. No, Alfred / No, Alfred! SCOTTY! Don't take –

Scotty Get off of her, Alfred. Motherfucker! You get the fuck away from my sister.

He fires the Nerf water gun at an imaginary Alfred.

Sam Leave me alone! Don't take / me. Don't take me.

Scotty What do you think you're doing, Swartzfatter? Get the hell away from my sister. You want to mess with my gun? I'll kill you. You don't take my sister. You can't take / anything. Go fucking drown in our pool, bitch!

Sam Don't take me. Don't take me. Don't take / me. Don't –

Scotty Boom, bitch!

He's gone. You're safe. He can't take my sister.

He starts to laugh, and they laugh together.

Sam I need a gun. I have to.

Scotty If I get you one, can I live here?

I need a permanent address for, uh, a new job. To save up. Hawaii?

Sam Show me the gun.

Scotty Maybe we should get you an animal or something.

Sam Uh, Axel?!

Scotty That bunny taught us to be fucking careful with the air rifle!

Sam I know you have one now. Give it up. What model? If it's a Glock 21 or, Jesus, a Beretta. A Berrreeettttaaa. Hey, I'll take anything! I love them all equally, I would never / choose –

He grabs her water gun and starts to run with his water gun too.

Scotty You really really want a gun?

Sam You'll break it!

Scotty First one in the pool wins! Go!

Sam I don't want to swim. My friends like swimming.

He beats her to the 'backyard' which is **Sam** *and* **John***'s room. She grabs her Nerf gun from him and he squirts her with his water gun. He gets her in the face and she starts to cough.* **John** *has just got into bed.*

Sam Not in the face! Arhhh. Don't fucking do that!

Scotty *jumps on the bed and dances around* **John**. **Sam** *tries to get all the water off of her face.*

John What the hell is going on?

Sam Nothing / nothing.

Scotty We were / goofing.

John You're getting me wet. Goddamn it, I didn't think we were babysitting. It's late.

He sees **Sam***'s bullet wound openly out.*

John Babe. That makes me sad.

Sam Don't look at it then

Scotty Don't you miss having fun?

John I have fun.

Scotty Jump on the bed, then.

He jumps on the bed around **John**.

Scotty Jump!

JUMP! Stop being so uptight. I miss you, Johnny!

He tries to pull **John** *up playfully.* **John** *doesn't move.*

Sam Yeah! Scotty could move back / in like old times!

Scotty Hey wait, you guys can talk about it / later.

John This isn't that big a place, I don't – Do you want to end up being forty on our couch?

Scotty I wanna be friends, dude.

John I didn't say I didn't.

Scotty But you don't /

Sam Remember the three of us in a bed. One bottle of champagne?

John If you really thought about getting off the guns, well then maybe we could think about / rebuilding things.

Scotty Jesus, I don't need help. It's normal /

John You're addicted to them, man.

Scotty I'm proud and / free.

John And it's your right and it's not hurting anyone else. I was there. And everyone else has them, everyone else is fine. So of course I'm fine. But when you decide to take the weight of that thing off of your hip and you're not walking around with it every single second like the rest of these zombies, so much more is possible. Sure, being outside, going to the mall, the bar, there's a real adjustment period feeling on edge but when you're over here where I'm standing / then you'll –

Sam There's no shame, Scotty.

John Stop playing guns around my house and stop setting a bad example like the rest of society.

Scotty She wants the gun!

Sam Hey / listen I was –

John Are you drunk?

Scotty No.

John Are you high?

Scotty Not right now.

John I'm going to bed /

Scotty And I told her no, not unless you were like awesome possum with it. I'm being respectful.

Sam I wouldn't even take it anywhere. I'd have it sitting in the bedside table. Just want to know I have one if I need it. I won't use it. And you don't have to see it or use it or you can if you want.

John God, you're right, Scotty. You didn't put any ideas in her head.

Sam It's my idea, this is my idea.

John It was your idea to get rid of them all.

Scotty I don't wanna get in the middle of this.

John You seem like you're enjoying it.

Scotty No, I'm saying my sister should be able to do whatever she wants.

Sam And I do / do what I want.

Scotty But sure jumping on a bed is kinda fun.

Sam I've changed my mind, okay. Let's talk about it.

Scotty I don't know why you need to get his permission.

John *starts to jump on the bed.* **John** *and* **Scotty** *jump on the bed staring at each other.*

John We've made a decision for our safety. Now drop it.

Scotty I could poke my finger through her gaping shoulder, / John.

Sam / It's not that big.

Scotty Just because you screwed up doesn't mean she will.

John Just because you're in my house doesn't mean I won't hit you.

Scotty Are you still scared of birds?

He starts to squawk. **John** *pushes* **Scotty** *off the bed.*

Sam Okay. Okay. It was a stupid idea. Forget it. We had a couple of drinks.

Scotty And now I'm the bad guy. Again.

Sam *shoots both* **Scotty** *and* **John** *with her Nerf gun.*

Sam Fuck you and fuck you. Make up. You're friends.

John Sam.

Scotty Hey, I'm trying. And he did that.

Sam Maybe you don't mention / the birds.

John I've shot them – I'm not scared of / birds, okay.

Sam Fuck! Have either of you made four-course chicken nugget dinners every night while wearing a fucking dead child's clothes and heels two sizes too big? He'd hit his knife on his glass and I'd put more and more ketchup on his plate. All while the world / didn't even –

John / Sam. Please.

Sam Mr Corbett wasn't my hero. That girl is going to die and if there are copycats and someone wants to / hurt us.

John It's a no. Sam, it's a no. She's not going to die, we have to hope / they'll –

Sam They're showing her picture on TV. She's all over the internet . . . C'mon what's he gonna do to her?!

She jumps higher and higher on the bed and falls.

Scene Eight

Day Five/Six, Middle of the Night (Sunday/Monday)

Sam *and* **John***'s bedroom.*

Sam *is asleep; this is the first time we've ever seen her actually sleeping.*

John (*whispers*) You're safe. I love you. I love you. I love you. Is this okay?

He starts to reach under the covers to her body. He starts pulling her underwear down to go down on her.

She jumps up and in under eight seconds she reaches for the Nerf gun in her bedside table. She points it at him.

Sam What the fuck?

John I thought I'd surprise / you.

Sam What the . . . were / you trying to . . .?

John You said soon? It was your favourite and you'd do a happy cry when I'd wake you up / going down on you so –

Sam I can't – not / no.

John I'm sorry. I thought you – I wanted you to feel good, that's it.

Sam I can't – we can't do that, if we lose ourselves we're not safe anymore / we can't –

John I thought if I surprised you like we – showed you how hot – you know it's been six / months.

Sam Six months. I know. You say it every day. You might as well say it's been six months, four days, seven hours, twenty-two minutes and fourteen seconds.

You wanna fuck, get me a gun.

John I promise it will be so much better with both of our hands free . . .

She goes to the bathroom with her Nerf gun.

John I don't want to work you up. I don't. I wasn't trying to –

Sam That was not okay.

John You're right. I'm sorry.

Um uh . . .

. . . So what's the latest with the case?

Sam Don't act interested now.

John (*reading from his phone*) Cindy Jordan begged Jessica to play violin for her, even though she disliked practising, after school on Tuesday. Although Jessica's phone was found in her room, she or her abductor did take her violin with her, leaving her bow behind / and –

Sam Thanks, didn't know that already.

John Who do you think did it?

Sam

She turns the shower on.

John Are you taking a shower? That's good.

Are you okay? I'm sorry. I am, I'm really sorry. It was stupid. Here. Shoot me. Would that make you feel better?

He goes to her in the bathroom.

John Shoot me.

She flushes the toilet and walks into the living room with the Nerf gun.

John Wait. Little arm!

He turns the shower off.

She twists the barrel so it makes a clicking sound and starts to wake **Scotty** *up.*

Sam Scotty? Scotty? Scotty? / Scotty.

Scotty Shit. You scared me.

Sam Can I sleep in here?

Scotty Did I get you in trouble?

Sam You're getting me a gun. That's what's happening.

Scotty Damn /

Sam Maybe we can go to Hawaii soon.

Scotty I'm not trying to break up a marriage here. I'm just looking for a place to crash.

Sam You're getting me a gun.

Can you get in the chair?

Scotty I'm sleeping.

Sam I need to do another now.

Scotty We got him, remember. It was good.

Sam The one in the chair.

Scotty

Sam Please.

He gets up and sits in the chair.

Sam I'm me and you're / him and I'm at his place.

Scotty I don't wanna be him.

Sam You don't have to say anything, okay.

Scotty

She starts to circle him in the chair with her Nerf gun.

Sam I'm chained to the wall. You take me to the kitchen and chain me there. I make you chicken nuggets for breakfast. You clink the glass. More ketchup. More ketchup. You rub your dirty clothes in my face. I clean them by hand.

Fold. Fold. Fold. More chicken nuggets. You chain me to the wall near the bathroom. You make me get in the tub in the dead child's clothes and wash your hair. I'm soaking wet. I shiver. More chicken nuggets. More ketchup. You tell me no one will ever wear my clothes because. It's night and you chain me to the wall in the basement.

He says

I'm

Coming

For

You.

I'll have you. I'll hurt you.

I stay awake all night. I wait. The silence. I wait. My eye just keeps twitching.

You

Never

Come.

It's morning. I'm chained to the wall still. You take me to the kitchen and chain me there.

You fucking broke my heart. And I'm going to fucking break your skull. With one bullet.

Say goodbye. BOOM.

She shoots her Nerf gun at his head.

Scotty Owww!

She grabs a plate on the coffee table and smashes it.

Scotty *jumps.*

Scotty / wow!

Sam OOOkkay.

John (*from the other room*) WHAT HAPPENED?

Scotty I shit – I knocked a plate over!

John SAM?!

Sam (*to* **Scotty**) Asshole. We're cleaning it up.

Sam *and* **Scotty** *wait to hear more from* **John** *but he quiets down.*

Scotty You know I love you, don't you?

Sam Why'd you say that?

Scotty Because I haven't.

He goes to clean up the plate.

Sam I'll get it later. Did Mom email you to say / that or something?

Scotty I know I'm tough but I got a human heart in here too.

Sam I'll hide it, okay. We could put the gun somewhere secret.

Scotty Or you can put it somewhere safe and accessible.

Sam No, no, no, I want to know where it is and that it's mine. That it's real. I know that was a lot right there but I just needed to get it out. I'm totally stable I'm . . . mourning Jessica's death.

Scotty What she fucking died? They found the body?

Sam Nah, I just know they will.

Scotty Maybe we turn off the Google Alerts, for a day?

Sam I know it's Beard. She trusts him. I bet they're kissing right now.

Scotty You're so lucky he didn't kiss you.

Sam Totally. Now he's on her left shoulder, and then kissing right down the whole of her / arm to her fingertips. It's like she's a mannequin. She knows she's . . .

Scotty Sam.

Sam

Scotty Sam, snap out of it.

Sam Do you think I'm crazy?

Scotty No. Dude, it's not wrong. I want my guns and no one tried to kidnap me. I'd have them stapled to me if I went through what you did. You're a gun girl. I get that.

Sam I'll take you to Hawaii if you come through. All-inclusive pass and shit.

Scotty Yeah?

Sam And I'd even swim. Do the breaststroke. We'd put our heads under and hold our breath.

I want us to go back to the old house on Franklin Street and swim one day.

Scotty Really?

Sam That makes me want to shit myself just thinking about it. Jesus if we could –

Scotty . . . So you know I'm good for it.

He hands her a box. They both hold it.

Sam Oh my God.

Her knees go weak.

Sam The weight.

Scotty Yeah.

Sam The smell.

Scotty I love it, too. Only in an emergency. Promise?

Sam I wanna hold them.

Scotty Don't open until saggy balls goes to the bar.

Sam I know.

He taps the couch to get her to lie down.

Scotty Do you want some socks?

Sam They don't smell that bad.

Scotty Oh yeah they do.

He puts socks on her feet.

Sam Thank you so much.

They lie down on the couch as top and tail. It is quiet and calm.

Scene Nine

Day Six, Morning (Monday)

In **Sam** *and* **John***'s bedroom.* **John** *is about to leave for work but stops himself. He goes to his closet. He opens it. He closes it. He opens it.*

John Fuck it.

He grabs his Nerf gun from the closet and points it. He jumps on and off the bed with it. He stuffs it into the front of his trousers. His shoulders drop. He touches it. He stops himself.

John (*quietly*) No gun, more fun. No gun, more fun. No. Shit, shit. John, you're okay, man. Fuck. You got this.

He goes to put it back. No, no yet. He looks in the mirror and poses. He tosses it up in the air, spins and goes to catch it but misses. He tries again and misses.

He puts it back in the closet. He walks into the living room and leaves a note next to **Sam** *pretending to sleep. It says, 'I'm sorry. I love you.' He leaves.*

In the living room: **Sam** *opens her eyes, reads the note and crinkles it up. She takes the box to the bedroom.*

The sun is shining and this is the first time we've seen full daylight. It's painfully bright.

She opens the box. It is a package of bullets.

Sam One, two, three, four, five, six, seven, eight, nine, ten, eleven, twelve, thirteen, fourteen, fifteen, sixteen, seventeen, eighteen, nineteen, twenty, twenty-one, twenty-two –

There is a sound of a car speeding past outside. She gets several news alert notifications on her phone about the case.

Twenty-one, wait – twenty, twenty, twenty –

She pushes them all into the same pile and starts again.

One, two, three, four, five, six, seven, eight, nine, ten, eleven, twelve, thirteen, fourteen, fifteen, sixteen, seventeen, eighteen, nineteen, twenty, twenty-one, twenty-two, twenty-three, twenty-four, twenty-five, twenty-six, twenty-seven, twenty-eight, twenty-nine, thirty.

She lays down and kisses the bullets, rolling around with them. She puts one in her pocket.

Scene Ten

Day Seven/Eight, Middle of the Night (Tuesday/ Wednesday)

The living room.

Scotty *sits in the living room whilst the news plays.* **Rebecca Roberts** *wears a 'Search for Jessica Jordan' t-shirt.*

Rebecca Roberts It has now been nine days since the disappearance of thirteen-year-old Jessica Jordan. We all continue to pray for a miracle. Kristy Cooper has the latest.

Scotty *stares at a stuffed whitetail deer with a t-shirt on it that says 'Budweiser'. He undresses the deer, pulls out a knife and tears open the middle of its belly and pulls out the stuffing.*

Kristy Cooper *also wears a 'Search for Jessica Jordan' t-shirt.*

Kristy Cooper Thanks, Rebecca, great t-shirt. The Jordan family and community continues to hold out hope that Jessica will be found in time to compete in the talent competition next Thursday evening. Her music teacher, Jeff Bergman, shared that she was planning to play 'Somewhere Over the Rainbow'.

Detective Cunningham has also confirmed that Miss Winnie and Beard have been engaging in a sexual relationship. This is following the discovery of Jessica's fingerprints on the front seat and her ballet shoes in the back seat of Beard's 2015 Nissan Frontier King Cab S truck.

Scotty *pulls out a gun from behind the back of his pants. He kisses it, and puts it inside the deer's belly. He puts the stuffing around it, pins the opening in the stomach back together and places the t-shirt over the top of the deer.*

He picks up the deer, holds it on his hip and walks out of the house to the backyard.

Scene Eleven

Day Eight, Early Evening (Wednesday)

Scotty *walks into* **Sam** *and* **John***'s bedroom with two beers in his hand.*

Scotty Oh. Sorry, thought Sam was in here.

John Nope.

Scotty Ah. Don't wanna bother you.

John Okay.

Scotty Uh, peace offering, dude?

John Thanks for bringing me one of my beers. What do you wanna say?

Scotty I – well. Genevieve got good results on her SATs which is great news so / I –

John Okay. What's your thing with jailbait?

Scotty Like I said don't wanna bother you.

John What is it?

Scotty Yeah. So she was going to come over tonight. Wanted to check it was cool.

John It's not.

Scotty I appreciate you having me stay. I really do.

He puts his hand out to **John**. **John** *does not reciprocate.*

Scotty I get it, I'll do the dishes for the next week. Totally fair. Do you have a dishwasher?

John Next time Sam comes in the living room, send her back in here. Somehow every time I wake up, she's in there with you. What are you doing?

Scotty She wanted to talk.

John She was getting better. And then you showed up.

He ruffles through his things, looking for something.

Scotty There's nothing wrong with her.

John I know there's not.

He finds his book about addiction and recovery.

Scotty You think there is.

John Chapter Four. I marked it.

Don't eat the beef jerky.

I've read about this and right here – you're masking your discontentment at how you aren't happy and couldn't break through like we have, together.

Scotty All of a sudden you stop partying and shooting and you think you're better than me?

John I can't have a gun, but other people can. You're just not one of those people.

Scotty I smell jealousy!

John You're trying to fuck with me.

Scotty Dude, I don't know what you're talking about. Sure, the bird thing was a low blow. But it's funny.

John You're going to bullshit me, Scotty? How long have we known each other.

Scotty I'm not bullshitting you.

John I don't care that you sell weed and cocaine, I don't care that you make fun of me. I don't care that you can't take care of yourself and we have to. I don't really because I know it makes Sam happy. But I do care about a goddamn bullet in my house.

Scotty . . . I don't know what you're talking about.

John I thought I laid out the rules of our programme / and staying here.

Scotty She's terrified with everything happening and I, listen – I thought one bullet wouldn't hurt anything.

John *pushes* **Scotty** *against the wall with force.*

Scotty Ow, wow / wow, let go.

John Don't even think about giving her anything else. Don't even think about it for one more fucking second.

Scotty I know.

John So where's the gun?

Scotty In the storage locker.

John All of them?

Scotty Yeah.

John There's no gun to go with the bullets for her?

Scotty There's no gun. Unless what you're saying is maybe you want one and I mean I could / maybe –

John . . . No! No guns.

Scotty More fun!

John *punches* **Scotty** *in the stomach.*

John Where's the gun?

Scotty I won't get it for her.

John If I find a gun / I'm not joking I'll –

Scotty You won't find one. You won't.

John I won't find a gun?

Scotty No.

John Great.

Cheers, then.

John *and* **Scotty** *clink beers.*

John Don't fucking make me the fucking bad guy.

Scotty Yeah, I get it.

Scene Twelve

Day Eight, Evening (Wednesday)

In the living room. **Scotty** *takes his Nerf guns off the wall.*

Scotty (*on the phone*) Ah, babe you tell me if that goddamn prick says one more thing about your ass in the cafeteria. I'll come stomp his face.

Yeah, I'll get you some Smirnoff Ice for the party later.

Sam You better not have proposed to Genevieve.

Scotty No.

Sam She's not pregnant is she?

Scotty No, no.

Sam Oh shit, did you get your job back?

Scotty Definitely not.

Sam *shoots her Nerf gun at him.*

Sam Well, I'm not gonna stop shooting you till you tell me what you're doing.

He catches the darts and hands them to her.

Scotty Thanks for letting me crash this long, I'm moving / out.

Sam Nooooo you're not going anywhere, you can't leave.

Scotty He found the bullet.

Sam Fuck. Fuck / Fuck. Fuck.

Scotty What were you thinking / leaving

Sam / It's my fault.

Scotty . . . one out like that? You promised.

Sam It got so warm in my hand. Felt like there was life in there. I'll be more careful

Scotty I'm outta here.

Sam Please / please.

Scotty I can't keep getting in trouble.

Sam How'd you get in trouble? What'd he do?

Scotty You only want me here / for the –

Sam Honestly, I don't want you to do anything you're not comfortable with. You don't have to do it.

Scotty Oh, really?

Sam Yeah, I don't have to have one, I'd like one, ya know. I don't think about them like I used to. It's not compulsive.

Scotty I told him I wasn't giving you a gun. So . . . I'm not.

Sam Okay, I get it.

You're not.

Cool.

Scotty It's not fun being the bad guy that gets caught all the time. I need a fucking change.

Sam You're not. I'll be fine. No obligation to do it.

Scotty Uh huh.

Sam I never broke a plate before – that was – it just all mounted up. Fluke, you know.

Scotty . . . Okay.

Sam I'll figure it out when she dies, I'll have to be fine. Sure I'm scared every single moment and can't think about anything else and all my everything is coming back but I'm not making you do something like that that you don't 100 per cent want to do.

Scotty

Sam This is my problem not yours . . . my shit to get over.

Scotty (*quietly*) Fuck . . .

Go to the elm tree.

Sam Oh my God what? Louder!

Scotty It's there now.

(*Whispers and hardly audible.*) The elm tree . . .

Sam SCOTTY! Oh my God. I love you! I might have even – I was around it – Ah, this is so exciting.

Scotty Only for emergencies. Please don't be stupid – no getting it this weekend immediately – he can't know. He can't. For me, okay? Sam?! It's for your safety, that's it.

Sam Yeah, yeah I know.

Scotty He can't know.

She puts one of his Nerf guns back on the wall.

Sam Okay, so new one. I'm me. And you're him /

Scotty Hey, hey, wait / no, no, no, I don't wanna –

Sam You stand there. It's the third day / in the house.

Scotty We're not doing it

She puts her Nerf gun in his hands.

Sam I'm chained / to the wall and you're pointing the gun at me and then –

Scotty Listen!

He drops the Nerf gun.

Sam You come / towards me and say, 'Wear these clothes, they might make you look prettier'.

Scotty No.

. . . He said that?

She grabs a child-like dress from her bag and starts to puts it on over her clothes. It's clearly too small.

Scotty Sam! Sam. No! We're not doing it.

He takes the dress from her.

Scene Thirteen

Day Eight, Late Night (Wednesday)

John *and* **Sam**'*s bedroom.* **John** *is holding the bullet.*

Sam Hand it to me? Babe?

John How'd he break you?

Sam It's not his fault. It was my idea.

John To have a bullet? A full pack of them?

Sam Just for holding. They're warm.

John What did I do wrong? I chose you.

Sam You love bullets. You said that they reminded you of solid raindrops. Remember?

John It doesn't matter.

Sam Remember what we used to do. When / we first got together?

John Sam, we have to be strong. We're / strong.

Sam Do you remember?

John Sam / please.

Sam You loved it. It made you so hard.

Can you get hard for me?

John Uh, of course. I can get the hardest anyone has ever been hard ever so hard for you.

Sam Hand me the bullet, then.

John . . . noooo. I'm not going to get hard right now we are going to shrink, bullets are not sexy, they're not sexy.

She puts her hand out.

Sam If Mr Corbett didn't have a gun . . . I wouldn't be here. Show me I'm still here.

John This is a little, a little back step and we can get turned around. Let's read a chapter aloud from / the book

Sam It's not / an addiction.

John . . . and then let's try to make love.

Sam I want to now and this is embarrassing asking you /

John I told you there might be relapses and I'm identifying that this is a this is a – yeah /

Sam She's going to die. That beautiful little girl that plays the violin is going to die. Just make me feel alive / right now.

John The police will find her.

Sam They didn't find me, they didn't / look.

John You survived.

Sam You laughed at that picture of me.

John What? No, I didn't laugh, you were – it was . . .

She puts her hand out again. He puts the bullet inside her hand. She puts his hand on hers to feel the heat. She puts the bullet on the bedside table.

Sam Look at it.

John Yeah, it's there.

Sam No, really look at it.

She turns his face to stare at it.

Sam Do you know what today is?

John Happy one-year anniversary. Wife.

She kisses his hard.

Sam You're hard already.

John We've worked to get away / from this.

Sam I'm ready. Really ready.

John Now?

Sam Let me have it there. Watching us, sparkling.

John I don't want that to be the only reason.

Sam C'mon.

John This is the last time it's sitting there. Promise?

She moves his face so that they are both staring at the bullet.

Sam Touch me.

John It can't become a habit.

Sam Kiss my arm and / then I want.

John Do I make you feel really safe and warm? I'm gonna make love to you, Sam.

Sam Okay but now bang me!

They laugh and then look at the bullet. They kiss and begin to make love.

Scene Fourteen

Day Ten, Early Morning (Friday)

John *and* **Sam***'s bedroom. It's so early, it's still dark outside.*

Sam *pees and goes back into the bedroom.* **John** *walks into the bedroom with a tub of vanilla ice cream and two spoons.*

He gives her a high five.

John We are very very very good at making love.

Sam Yeah. Shit, what time is it?

John 5 a.m. Vanilla ice cream, my queen?

She takes the ice cream. They eat from the tub together.

Sam Thank youuuu.

John Remember in those first three months we always had ice cream before bed and we'd wake up in the middle of the night with wet spots in bed from it melting?

Sam And you thought it was just / some cum stains.

John I love you.

Sam I love you too.

John I think that was the last time with the bullet.

Sam Yeah we got it out of our systems on the eighth time.

John Did you pee?

Sam Yep.

John Great. I don't want you get a UTI again.

She turns the TV on.

John Heyyy.

Sam Shhh . . .

John We should turn it off. Get a bit more sleep.

Sam I'll read it on my phone if we don't watch it / here.

John We should turn it off.

Sam . . . Okay.

John Let's turn it off. Practising restraint together.

He puts her fingers on the remote and they turn it off.

John How about I put your phone on this side too?

She gives him her phone.

John Good girl. Did I make you orgasm?

Sam . . .

She forces a smile. He gives her a thumbs up and turns off the lamp for them to go to sleep.

When he is fully asleep, she gets out of bed with her Nerf gun. She looks out the window to the elm tree in the backyard.

Sam I'm coming.

Scene Fifteen

Day Ten, Morning (Friday)

It is very early in the morning and, as the scene goes on, it becomes brighter and brighter.

Sam *lies in bed pretending to be asleep.*

John Babe, you don't wanna be late.

Sam (*sleepily*) Where you going now?

John Working out. I gotta stay sexy for you.

He leaves.

Sam I fall asleep in a red blanket and I wake up. I look outside. He's gone. It's dark but there's so much light.

Kristy Cooper If you have just joined us, we bring you breaking news in the case of Jessica Jordan, the Butler student who has been missing for the past eleven days. Jessica's sister, Chloe Jordan, remembered a brief conversation she had with Jessica a few weeks ago when she mentioned that her music teacher Jeff Bergman encouraged her to practise very hard for the talent show.

Sam I have to go outside. Can I go outside? It's outside.

Kristy Cooper And if she did, he'd buy her a new bow to perform with.

Sam I go to the back yard. Like he said.

Kristy Cooper We have confirmed with the Butler Township Police Department that

Sam I feel the squishy soil and walk on leaves. I take off my shoes.

Kristy Cooper . . . Jeff Bergman has been named as a suspect and is currently in police custody for questioning.

Sam I look up at the elm tree and I look down to its left side. I dig. I dig. I dig. I dig.

Kristy Cooper A full search at his residence is taking place for clues that may lead us to Jessica's location and we –

Sam I dig.

Kristy Cooper Oh – I am receiving a live update from the authorities, coming live, breaking news /

Sam Diiiiiiing, two feet under the elm tree. On the left-hand side. Tucked inside is something stuffed. It's a whitetail deer.

Kristy Cooper I am being told that Butler resident Cookie Caper was walking her dog Cupcake in Butler Memorial Park near the creek when Cupcake couldn't stop barking and /

Sam *digs out the stuffed deer.*

Sam I hold him but I don't stop digging.

Kristy Cooper Cookie found a violin bow buried near the creek, and she walked towards the water to discover /

Sam *dusts off the deer, lifts its shirt up and unpins its stomach.*

Sam I rip, I dig, I rip, I dig.

Kristy Cooper A tragic ending

Sam I dig, dig, dig, dig out the deer's belly.

Kristy Cooper . . . to the investigation.

Sam *throws out the stuffing and pulls out a gun. It is a gun.*

Sam And

There

She

Is.

She cocks back the gun.

Kristy Cooper Jessica Jordan's body has been found in the Butler Memorial Park Creek. They estimate her to have been in the water for at least seventy-two hours. We are being told that she suffered an impact to the head, with signs of sexual assault and a significant amount of water in the lungs suggesting that drowning may have been the cause of death. A full report will be carried out in the following days and we will / confirm.

Sam *raises her gun up to the sky.*

Music plays and starts to drown out the news.

She is contained but then she starts to move. It builds to an intense dance with her gun. It is not necessarily good, but it is honest, free and happy.

Scene Sixteen

Day Ten, Morning (Friday)

Sam *sits on the floor of the bedroom. She cleans her gun.*

Her phone starts to ring. She silences it. It rings again.

Sam (*on phone*) Oh, hi Becky. Yeah, sorry. I've been meaning to – I've just been in the bathroom throwing up.

Yeah, yeah. I emailed my doctor's note last week. Oh.

I'll resend it, of course.

She goes to spray her gun again but nothing comes out.

I'll be back on Monday.

She gets more gun cleaner. She cleans it again.

Thanks, Becky. Sorry. Bye.

She coughs.

Bye.

She hangs up.

Just me and you today.

She loads the gun. She unloads the gun.

You sound great.

She dresses the gun up with a sock and frills. She moves it around like a toy doll.

My beautiful little girl.

Jessica.

She positions 'Jessica' back inside the deer's belly. She puts the deer's shirt back on, places it on her hip and grabs her keys. She opens the door, feels a breeze and one foot at a time walks out of the house for the first time in over a week.

Scene Seventeen

Day Ten, Early Evening (Friday)

John *looks for* **Scotty**.

John I can't get through to Sam. Has she answered your calls?

Scotty A bit clingy – I mean that was a joke – You talking to me now?

John They found Jessica Jordan's body.

Scotty Fuck / what?

John Yeah, Butler Memorial Park.

Scotty I'm not gonna sell there anymore.

John Do you know where Sam is? Have you talked to her today? She's usually home by now.

Scotty I'll, uh, I'll call her and I'll drive by the Courthouse to check for her car.

John *tries to call* **Sam**. *Nope. Straight to voicemail.* **Scotty** *tries. Nope, voicemail too.*

Scotty *starts to go.*

John No, no, you gotta stay here.

Scotty But maybe we'll cover more ground if you're /

John I'm not gonna hit you. Calm down.

Scotty That's not what I –

John Maybe she doesn't know yet.

Scotty Dude.

John Well, when things are bad, she likes to be alone, in bed with dirty socks.

Scotty But food calms her down. That's her chill.

John What can she do with a bullet on its own? She wouldn't do anything crazy, right?

Scotty No, no, she won't, she can't do anything

John She might cry, but that's okay. I can deal with that. She should cry.

Scotty Oh God that cry face, am I right!

John It's not funny but it's funny, you know?

Scotty Looks like she's pushing out a big turd.

Scotty *does the face and then* **John** *does it with him. They laugh.*

Scotty They find out who did it?

John Music teacher. Bergman.

Scotty Glad I never learned an instrument.

John I can't believe she died.

Scotty Sam knew she would.

John She thinks everyone is going to die.

You know, I'm gonna help you out, you can stay a few more nights.

Scotty Nah, I'm heading out tomorrow /

John No, you're staying.

Scotty You're scared?

Sam *walks in the house with the deer on her hip.*

John Hey, babe! (*To* **Scotty**.) Order a pizza now.

Guess what . . .

Sam / Uhh

John We're getting a pizza! How's that sound? Do you want your PJs and socks before it comes?

Sam Great, I'm starving. (*To* **John**.) Why are you / home now?

Scotty (*on the phone*) Hi, can I order a pizza?

John (*to* **Sam**) You want pepperoni?

Scotty Yeah, Hawaiian and spicy pepperoni. Two larges. Yep, that's it / Shady Road. 16801. Great. Yep, that's the card.

John Did you have a good day?

Sam Yeah, it was fine.

John Good. Good. Who's your sidekick there?

Scotty Pizza pizza pizza will be here in thirty minutes.

John Wanna sit down?

Sam You're acting weird.

John Where's your Nerf?

Sam She's here.

John Good. Hold onto it. We want to talk to you and we're both / here

Scotty Jessica Jordan died. They found her / body.

Sam body at Butler Memorial Park. I know, I told you she'd die.

John Oh.

Sam Sucks. It's tragic but. It happened.

Scotty Yeah, it's a lot and –

John Have you cried?

Sam I feel bad for the family. But I mean, honestly, once they put her picture up and he knew everyone was looking for her, I mean goner. Done for. And that Jeff Bergman was in love with her.

John Sam, she's really gone.

Sam *goes to the fridge.*

Scotty Yeah, it's over.

Sam *opens a beer and chugs it.*

She grabs two more beers and goes to throw them at **John** *and* **Scotty**.

John Sam

Scotty / Uh.

John No / thanks.

Sam We're drinking tonight. Me and my boys.

John Maybe next weekend / instead?

Sam *kisses* **John** *hard.*

John You know, I think, I'm sure you're upset and sometimes when you drink, well, alcohol can make you sad, it's a depressant / after all.

Sam Scotty, I just saw that cat on the stoop! Let's name him.

Scotty Za, like pizza?

Sam Everyone at work said I looked really nice today. And I do. I feel nice. Do you have any weed, Scotty? It's a sad time but think about how lucky we are.

John Sam . . .

Sam (*mockingly*) John . . .

John You can talk to us.

Sam Oh I gotta pee, shouldn't break the seal yet but whatever.

She goes to the bathroom with the deer and the beer.

John When there's a missing or dead, uh, are we supposed to, I dunno.

Scotty Let's go with it. She's gotta lead us and show us what she needs right now.

John Okay, I'm glad you're here.

Scotty *puts out his hand.* **John** *reciprocates.*

John*'s phone vibrates. He reads.*

John Fuck, fuck, fuck.

Scotty What happened?

John They need me at Bernard's. Two people didn't show up tonight.

Scotty Jobs are stupid.

John . . . Um should we take her?

Scotty No way.

John Okay.

Then I should stay

Scotty Whatever.

John Uhhh . . .

Scotty

John'*s phone starts to ring.*

John . . . Shit. Can you take care of her?

Scotty If I've gotta drink with her, I'll do that. I got ya.

John Scotty. Listen. Don't / listen.

Scotty You're asking me for a favour.

John (*on the phone*) Hey, just got your text. I'm in the truck and on my way.

He says goodbye to **Sam** *in the other room.* **Scotty** *chugs another beer.* **John** *rushes out of the house.*

Sam (*yells from the other room*) We're going swimming!

Scotty Hawaii? Yeah, when?

Sam No, Franklin Street.

She hands him another beer.

Sam Tonight.

He drinks.

Sam No one's home. I drove by earlier.

Scotty We're not going anywhere.

Sam Don't be – no. It's happening. It's happening.

Scotty

Sam John's out, home is empty, pool is open. Get your stuff, doofus.

Scotty Sam, we can't

She puts her beer out to him to cheers. He drinks instead.

Sam I feel fine, great. I do, really. Fuck Alfred. We're going to jump in the pool like we never got to that day. I'll hold my breath all the way and touch the bottom. I'll come up, and it'll be me and you.

Scotty Can't we watch a / movie.

Sam We'll get our lives back. Then we dry ourselves off and we move on. And Jessica can go back in the ground. Because no one can hurt me now.

Scotty Please.

Sam And that's because of you. You're a goddamn hero.

Please.

Please.

Pleasseeeeee.

Fuck it. I'm going on my own.

Scotty No, no / no.

Sam I'm doing it alone /

Scotty Well, I have to come – I was there – I'll come, okay / as long as you put it back afterwards.

Sam BLAH, BLAH, BLAH!

She flashes her swimsuit under her clothes to him.

Scotty I'm sorry I didn't hear you scream.

Sam Shut up and let's swim.

Scotty Let me get my gun.

Sam It's / here?

Scotty Shhh.

She grabs a bag, fills it with towels and throws her gun inside. They leave and travel to their old house on Franklin Street.

When they arrive they take off their clothes and are in their swimsuits. They put their guns in the side of their swimsuits as they approach the pool. They open up two beers, cheers and chug them. They do their secret handshake and may sing their song.

Scotty You better get a major splash. Like cannonball size.

Sam Okay?

Scotty Yeah.

She climbs up the pool ladder. He goes to climb up too.

Sam Wait, no, you're over there.

She climbs back down and goes to him.

She reaches into her bag and gets out headphones. She puts them on **Scotty***, takes him to 'his room' and turns him away from the pool.*

She climbs up the pool ladder on her own.

She stands on the edge of the diving board. She looks around. She jumps. Up. And. Down. She plugs her nose.

She keeps jumping up and down.

Is she going to?

She wipes her eyes.

Was she crying?

She stops jumping.

She's dead.

She starts to jump on the board again and she gets ready and she . . . jumps into the pool!

It is a big splash.

She holds her breath and touches the bottom of the pool. She comes up from the water in pure euphoria. She screams with joy.

She fucking did it!

Scene Eighteen

Day Ten/Eleven, Late Night (Friday/Saturday)

Sam *and* **Scotty** *try to get in the house but are struggling to find the light switch. They are drunk and can't stop laughing.*

Scotty MAJOR SPLASH?!

Sam I touched the bottom of the pool. Held my breath that long. I – I touched / the bottom.

Scotty I wish I coulda – I wanted to see. That big splasher.

Sam Splasher! I went deeeeeep!

Scotty Fuck, hit the / lights. This air conditioning is fucking Arctic, yo.

Sam I'm cold.

He waits for her to turn the lights on but she doesn't. He flips the switch.

Scotty Finally.

John *is sat on the couch on his phone waiting for them to come home.* **Sam** *and* **Scotty** *are dripping wet, holding their guns and a very wet deer.*

Now they really can't stop laughing. **Sam** *drops the deer.*

Scotty Ohhhhh / Shit.

Sam Ooopsss, my deer.

John You didn't get her a gun, Scotty?

Sam I'm / caught! Ooohhhh.

Scotty Busted!

John You got her a gun.

Scotty Dude.

Sam John, John, listen. I wanna say – tell / you, okay.

John Great, you're wasted.

Sam I'm not. That much.

John So you're creating the rules now? If you get drunk, you can have a gun and lie to me? Did you want me to go back to work tonight? You wanted me to catch you?

Sam I went swimming.

John You didn't want me to come along? I don't know the secret handshake?

Sam / John.

John I'm not a part of the cool club?

Sam It's not about – I had to finish something.

John You can't even follow the rules we created – that's all you had to do.

Scotty She never got to swim. She wanted to jump off the diving board / without Alfred.

John I fucking know. I know the story! (*To* **Scotty**.) Do you remember what I / said I'd do if you gave her a gun?

Sam It was my idea.

John I love you and know you needed your brother. So I let him stay. So I bought him Oreos, I let him fuck a high schooler in our home, but can't you see he just threw away everything we worked for?

Scotty Stop punishing her for something you did. She doesn't even hate you for it, dude.

John You want your sister to be shot again?

Scotty No, but she handled it fucking better / than you would.

John I'm gonna fuck you up.

Sam Okay, John, you're angry / I'm gonna explain.

Scotty I guess you're a lil' ol' fuck-up like me still. You tell her you never graduated / yet?

John / Don't.

Scotty That you punched / me?

Sam (*to* **John**) You fucking punched him?

(*To* **Scotty**.) Alright, Scotty, I think you better go.

John (*to* **Scotty**) Yeah, I think it's time for you to leave my house.

Scotty Isn't it Sam's house? Her money?

He gets on the couch and jumps on it. **John** *gets in* **Scotty**'*s face.* **Sam** *gets in between them.*

Sam Alright. Scotty, you've gotta leave. / Text Genevieve and see if you can crash there tonight.

John Pack it up.

Scotty I'm not leaving you.

Sam C'mon, text her.

John *takes* **Scotty**'*s gun with force.* **Scotty** *goes to grab it back from him but misses.*

Scotty Are you kidding me?

He gets in **John**'*s face.*

John Sam and I want you to go. C'mon, go.

Scotty Motherfucker! You get the fuck away from my sister.

John *points the gun at* **Scotty**. **Scotty** *puts his hands up.*

Sam Scotty.

Scotty Wow, okay. I'll fucking pack. Okay, okay.

John *keeps his gun pointed at* **Scotty**. **Scotty** *starts to throw things in his bag.*

Scotty No, No. I'm not going, I can't / let

Sam I said get out, Scotty.

Scotty I don't want / to –

Sam I don't need you anymore okay!

Scotty But –

Sam *points her gun at* **Scotty**.

Scotty *gives up and finishes packing.* **Sam** *and* **John** *point the guns at him and walk him to the door.*

Scotty *leaves.*

John *puts the gun down.*

John Jesus Christ.

Sam Pick up the gun.

Pick it up.

John

She puts her gun down.

John

Sam What are you scared of?

John Nothing – I'm not. I'm not.

He picks the gun back up.

Sam C'mere – Come

You stand there. I'll stand here.

I'm gonna be me / and –

John What do you mean you're gonna be you?

Sam We're at his place. I'm me and you're him /

John Sam, what are you / doing?

Sam I'm chained to the wall and / I –

John This is weird / and –

Sam I – Point the gun / at me.

John What? No!

Sam Listen to me.

John I'm not / doing that.

Sam Do you want me to make you dinner?

John No. I – / Sam can we –

Sam Chicken nuggets / again?

John Sam – no, no, no. Is this? I'm not doing this. This is stopping / right now. I – I – no, no

Sam Tell me you want more ketchup. More ketchup.

She gets a glass and a knife. She puts the glass in front of him and puts a knife in his hand. She makes him clink the glass.

John I'm not Alfred.

Sam Please?!

I'm me.

You're him. You're there eating chicken nuggets and I'm standing here / and –

John I'm not doing it /

I'm not doing it.

Sam Am I ever going to see my family again?

C'mon!

Am I ever going to see my family again?

John . . . No.

Never.

Sam Are people

are they

looking for me?

John Uh . . .

No one is looking for you

Sam No. No. Everyone is.

There are a thousand people on the street, all in, in a line, looking.

Yelling out, 'Sam! Sam!'

John Yeah, and there are search dogs and people are crying.

Sam Yeah.

John You're a pillar of the Butler community.

Sam I am.

John You're all over the internet, TV, there's a huge investigation.

You're so beautiful, everyone can't get enough.

Sam Really?

John Ew, this dinner's disgusting. What's wrong with you?

Sam I made you what you liked. What you loved.

John It's fucking shit!

Sam / I'm sorry.

John Well, now you're in trouble.

Sam You gonna lock me in the basement again?

John . . . Yes.

Sam You gonna switch off the lights?

John Yes.

Sam It's not bedtime /

John Now it is.

GO! NOW!

She goes.

Sam Are you coming for me?

John I'm not saying it again.

Sam Will you have me?

John I'll have you.

Sam Will you hurt me?

John I'll hurt you.

He turns the light off.

Goodnight, beautiful.

Sam *waits.*

And waits.

And waits.

And waits.

Sam (*whispers*) One

Two

Three

Four

Five

Six

Seven

Eight

One

Two

Three

Four

Five

Six

Seven

Eight

He looks for her.

John Sam?

Sam?

I'm gonna find you.

You can't hide.

I'm gonna –

I love you.

She is behind him.

I'm not scared.

He goes to her.

He closes his eyes and leans in to kiss her.

She quickly grabs the gun from 'Alfred' and pulls the trigger.

The gun doesn't fire.

They both jump.

There aren't any bullets.

Sam

John

Sam

The End.

Methuen Drama Modern Plays
include work by

Bola Agbaje
Edward Albee
Davey Anderson
Jean Anouilh
John Arden
Peter Barnes
Sebastian Barry
Alistair Beaton
Brendan Behan
Edward Bond
William Boyd
Bertolt Brecht
Howard Brenton
Amelia Bullmore
Anthony Burgess
Leo Butler
Jim Cartwright
Lolita Chakrabarti
Caryl Churchill
Lucinda Coxon
Curious Directive
Nick Darke
Shelagh Delaney
Ishy Din
Claire Dowie
David Edgar
David Eldridge
Dario Fo
Michael Frayn
John Godber
Paul Godfrey
James Graham
David Greig
John Guare
Mark Haddon
Peter Handke
David Harrower
Jonathan Harvey
Iain Heggie
Robert Holman
Caroline Horton
Terry Johnson
Sarah Kane
Barrie Keeffe
Doug Lucie
Anders Lustgarten
David Mamet
Patrick Marber
Martin McDonagh
Arthur Miller
D. C. Moore
Tom Murphy
Phyllis Nagy
Anthony Neilson
Peter Nichols
Joe Orton
Joe Penhall
Luigi Pirandello
Stephen Poliakoff
Lucy Prebble
Peter Quilter
Mark Ravenhill
Philip Ridley
Willy Russell
Jean-Paul Sartre
Sam Shepard
Martin Sherman
Wole Soyinka
Simon Stephens
Peter Straughan
Kate Tempest
Theatre Workshop
Judy Upton
Timberlake Wertenbaker
Roy Williams
Snoo Wilson
Frances Ya-Chu Cowhig
Benjamin Zephaniah

For a complete listing of
Methuen Drama titles, visit:

www.bloomsbury.com/drama

Follow us on Twitter and keep up to date
with our news and publications

@MethuenDrama